CW01512627

Original title:
Fragments of the Radiant Symphony

Author: Lan Donne
ISBN HARDBACK: 978-1-80565-079-9
ISBN PAPERBACK: 978-1-80565-282-3

Echoes of Twinkling Infinity

In a realm where stars waltz and play,
Whispers of dreams weave night into day.
Each glimmer a tale yet to unfold,
A cosmic embrace, both timid and bold.

Through unlimited skies, with hearts intertwined,
The laughter of worlds in harmony whined.
Chasing the echoes of memories dear,
In the dance of the cosmos, forever near.

Galaxies swirl like petals in bloom,
Two souls adrift, dispelling the gloom.
Beyond the horizons where wishes ignite,
We find our place in the tapestry bright.

Every heartbeat, a star's vibrant song,
Carving the path where we all belong.
In flickers of brilliance, a promise we see,
For echoes of twinkling infinity.

So breathe in the magic, let silence ensue,
In the void, there's a pulse both gentle and true.
The night holds its breath, and we lose all strife,
In the echoes of time, we discover our life.

Shadows of a Harmonic Odyssey

Beneath the moon's glow, shadows do sway,
Guided by whispers that lead us astray.
A path lined with secrets, both ancient and rare,
In shadows of twilight, adventures declare.

Wandering realms where the echoes reside,
The heartbeats of history, woven with pride.
From valleys of silence to mountains of song,
Each note a reminder of where we belong.

Through forests of memory, the past gently calls,
With voices of starlight that rise and that fall.
In every heartbeat, a tale finds its way,
Through shadows of time, we endlessly sway.

The moon smiles down on each daring quest,
In a dance of the night, we find our rest.
In harmony's glow, the stars shine so bright,
Casting shadows of dreams, igniting the night.

As visions take flight, in the silence we hear,
The symphony whispers, banishing fear.
In shadows, we wander, our spirits alive,
On this harmonic odyssey, we thrive.

The Pulse of Brilliant Whispers

In the hush of twilight's glow,
Where shadows dance and secrets flow,
A gentle breeze calls out the night,
In whispered tones, it takes its flight.

Among the stars, a chorus sings,
Of dreams that soar on silken wings,
Each note a thread of silken grace,
In the woven fabric of this place.

The heartbeats sync in hushed refrain,
With echoes soft, a sweetened pain,
Each pulse a story softly spun,
Of battles lost and victories won.

Beneath the moon, we find our way,
Through silver paths where fairies play,
The night unfolds its endless charms,
As whispers weave through outstretched arms.

And in the stillness, light reveals,
The truths that time and heart conceal,
In every breath, a promise holds,
The pulse of whispers, bright and bold.

Harmonies from a Distant Shore

Where waves caress the pebbled beach,
And salty winds begin to teach,
The melodies of ages past,
In echoes that forever last.

The seagulls cry, a timeless sound,
Where ocean's voice will ever pound,
A chorus born from deep blue tides,
Where mysteries of the sea abides.

Beneath the sun's warm, golden gaze,
The water glimmers in a haze,
Each ripple tells a tale untold,
Of shipwrecked dreams and treasures old.

Through salty air, a ballad flows,
Of mermaids' sighs and lovers' woes,
In every splash, a story found,
In harmonies, our hearts are bound.

As evening falls, the stars ignite,
A symphony of dark and light,
From distant shores, the music calls,
To hearts awake, where wonder sprawls.

Glowing Threads of Lost Songs

In quiet corners of the night,
Where shadows weave and dreams take flight,
A tapestry of voices hums,
With swaying notes of distant drums.

Through whispered woods where secrets dwell,
The glowing threads weave tales to tell,
Of laughter lost and wishes made,
In the fabric of the moonlit shade.

Like fireflies in a velvet sky,
Each spark ignites a soft goodbye,
With every glimmer, hearts entwine,
In songs of old, in notes divine.

A haunting tune drifts on the breeze,
Through rustling leaves and sleeping trees,
It calls us back to days long gone,
To echoes of a fleeting dawn.

Yet in this space, a hope remains,
In glowing threads, no loss retains,
For songs once sung shall rise anew,
In whispers soft, they will pursue.

A Symphony in Broken Light

In shards of dawn, the day breaks free,
A symphony from shadows, a plea,
Each beam a note, a vibrant spark,
In the ether, where dreams embark.

The colors blend, a canvas bright,
With hues that dance in gentle flight,
Through every crack, the sunlight spills,
A melody that softly thrills.

Yet in the fractures, stories hide,
Of journeys lost, of hearts that cried,
A bittersweet, harmonious blend,
Of hopes and fears that interwend.

With every step, the music swells,
In timeless echoes, laughter dwells,
For even broken, light can sing,
A symphony of everything.

So let us dance in fleeting rays,
And cherish all the broken ways,
For in the light that softly wanes,
A symphony of love remains.

Cadence of Lost Stars

In the quiet of night, whispers fly,
Dreams woven in time, like silver threads high.
Lost among echoes of shimmering light,
The cadence of stars bids farewell to the night.

Faint glimmers dance on the edge of despair,
Each heartbeat a wish, tangled strands of air.
Through shadows we wander, searching the past,
For moments once cherished, too fleeting to last.

A tapestry woven with laughter and tears,
Memories linger, defying the years.
In the silence, a promise softly hums,
That love's gentle music forever becomes.

Yet the night still calls with its haunting embrace,
A journey untouched, a familiar place.
In the cadence of stars, we find our way home,
Together, forever, wherever we roam.

Chasing Shadows of Light

Beneath the moon's glow, shadows take flight,
Dancing in corners, where dreams meet the night.
In pursuit of the glow that ignites our hearts,
We chase the soft shadows, where magic imparts.

With whispers of courage, we venture so far,
Each step a creation, a shimmering star.
In the dance of the dark, our spirits arise,
Illuminated hope in the depths of the skies.

Along paths of devotion, we wander and roam,
Finding light in the shadows, a glimpse of our home.
In the chase, we discover the dreams that ignite,
A world filled with wonder, while chasing the light.

So let us be fearless and dance through the haze,
For shadows are fleeting, lost in the phase.
With hearts intertwined and our spirits so bright,
We'll wander together, through chasing the light.

Fragmented Reverie

In pieces they scatter, memories unfold,
Fragments of moments, like stories retold.
Through whispers of time, in the echoes of dreams,
The reverie lingers, unraveling seams.

With each fragile shard, a truth we might find,
Reflections of laughter, of love intertwined.
In the quiet of dusk, as the stars come alive,
Our hearts beat in rhythm, our spirits survive.

Yet shadows may cloud what the heart can't deny,
In the dance of the night, the questions arise.
What magic awaits in this tapestry bright,
When we grasp the fragments and gather the light?

Through valleys of longing, we traverse the unknown,
Setting forth in fragments, no longer alone.
In the reverie's depth, we discover the art,
That even in pieces, love conquers the heart.

A Mosaic of Distant Echoes

Each echo a heartbeat, a story once told,
A mosaic of memories, a treasure of gold.
In whispers of time, across oceans and lands,
We gather the pieces, creating with hands.

Beneath the vast skies filled with starlit dreams,
We find our reflections in silvery beams.
A canvas of colors, woven from strife,
In echoes of laughter, we celebrate life.

With every connection, new paths intertwine,
From mountains to valleys, like branches that climb.
In the heart of the journey, love's essence remains,
In a mosaic of echoes, the spirit sustains.

So cherish the echoes, let them guide the way,
For in every whisper, the magic will stay.
Together creating, a masterpiece true,
In the dance of our stories, we find me and you.

Spectrums of Starlit Noise

In twilight's hush, the whispers glow,
A symphony in shadows flow.
Beneath the arch of sapphire skies,
The secrets of the night arise.

Harmonies in the silver streams,
Twinkling bright where darkness dreams.
Each star a note in cosmic song,
To the universe, we all belong.

A dance of light, a piquant thrill,
Echoes fade on winds that chill.
With every pulse, the starlight sings,
Of ancient tales that twilight brings.

Through veils of time, the echoes swell,
In quiet depths, a distant bell.
The cosmos weaves a tapestry,
In every note, a memory.

Let starlit music guide the way,
Through realms where shadows gently play.
For in the space where silence dwells,
The hearts of dreamers weave their spells.

A Tapestry of Melodic Fragments

Threads of sound entwined in air,
Notes adrift with casual flair.
Whispers gather, sharply defined,
In the heart, their paths aligned.

Rustling leaves in gentle tune,
Beneath the harvest moon's soft rune.
Melodies from hidden springs,
Awaken joy, the heart takes wings.

A snatch of laughter, a sigh, a tear,
Moments stitched, by memory sheer.
Patterns rise and twist apart,
Crafting echoes in the heart.

In every note, a story hides,
Of lonely journeys, ancient tides.
The weave of sound, a vibrant place,
Where time and spirit interlace.

From quiet seeds of dreams a-sown,
A kaleidoscope of dreams is grown.
With every brush of harmony,
A world unfolds in symphony.

Harmonious Glimpses of Eternity

Glimmers of light on velvet seas,
Whispers carried on the breeze.
Eternity's stories softly swirl,
In the curve of time, they twirl.

Ripples dance on a silver lake,
In a moment, futures awake.
Fleeting glimpses, echoes wide,
In the silt where memories bide.

Stars entwined in a graceful arc,
Spellbound dreams ignite the dark.
Harmonies blend in radiant hues,
Each one a thread of deeper clues.

As twilight fades to velvet night,
The cosmos hums with numinous light.
Each heartbeat matched to the skies,
A testament to the wise.

In reverie, the dreamers soar,
To weave the tales forevermore.
For in the heart of the cosmic sea,
Glows the pulse of eternity.

The Dance of Fractured Resonance

Fragments shift in tempest's breath,
Echoes haunt in dance with death.
Rhythms clash, collide and break,
In the silence, shadows quake.

Echoes linger, paths entwine,
In the chaos, secrets shine.
A ballet formed of fractured notes,
Tracing lines on time's thin coats.

Tattered dreams take flight anew,
Carried forth on skies so blue.
Each tremor tells of stories past,
Memories that forever last.

The broken chords weave wide and far,
Illuminated by a distant star.
In the swirling winds of disarray,
We find the beauty of decay.

Through jagged edges, hope can rise,
In every scar, a chance to prize.
For in the ruins, light does dance,
Weaving wonders in each chance.

Vibrations of the Ethereal Dream

In moonlit whispers, shadows sway,
The night unveils a mystic play.
With every sigh, the stars align,
Revealing secrets, pure, divine.

A tapestry of whispered thoughts,
In slumber's grasp, the world begot.
With colors spun from silken thread,
Awakening where dreams are bred.

Through twilight's lens, the echoes wane,
In spectral dances, joy and pain.
With every heartbeat, life expands,
In realms where only magic stands.

A gentle breeze, the touch of night,
In every flicker, find the light.
Where realms collide, and hearts ignite,
The dreamer soars, a wondrous flight.

In ethereal glow, the spirits hum,
Where every thought and wish is spun.
In the sacred fold of night's embrace,
Vibrations weave their timeless grace.

Luminous Rhythms Entrapped

In gardens where the moonbeams dance,
The leaves ignite in a mystic trance.
With every heartbeat, shadows play,
As dreams unfold in soft array.

A melody of whispers pure,
Entwined in stars, a gentle lure.
In cosmic silks, the notes arise,
A harmony that never dies.

Each twinkle tells a tale anew,
In rhythmic waves of silver hue.
With echoes lost in starlit streams,
The universe spins within our dreams.

Through silent nights, the secrets gleam,
Where darkness holds its sacred beam.
As shadows weave with light's embrace,
In luminous rhythms, time finds grace.

In every sigh, the night unfolds,
A tapestry of stories told.
Within each heartbeat, love is cast,
Entrapped in wonders, unsurpassed.

The Art of Starlit Silence

In velvet depths, where silence dwells,
Each starlit breath, a tale compels.
In quietude, the cosmos sighs,
A symphony beneath the skies.

The canvas stretched with shadows bold,
In silver whispers, truth unfolds.
Each moment drips like molten gold,
The art of night, a story told.

Through tranquil nights, the spirits weave,
In silent dreams, we dare to believe.
With every twinkle, secrets bloom,
As starlit silence lights the gloom.

In spaces vast, where echoes fade,
A tapestry of peace is laid.
With every heartbeat, time suspends,
In silent realms where the magic blends.

In tranquil shadows, the heart can find,
The art of silence, beautifully blind.
In every whisper, a journey starts,
A dance of starlight in longing hearts.

Notes Adrift in the Galaxy

In cosmic winds, where starlight flows,
Each note adrift, a longing grows.
With every twirl, the galaxies hum,
Creating magic as they come.

A symphony of worlds collide,
In endless notes, we take our ride.
Through stellar paths, the music bright,
Guides every wanderer in the night.

With distant echoes, the heart beats strong,
In harmony, we all belong.
A chorus formed from dreams and sighs,
In cosmic dances, we shall rise.

Through astral realms, the melodies soar,
Unlocking treasures, forevermore.
In every glance, the universe sings,
As souls entwine with otherworldly wings.

Amidst the stars, our spirits play,
In notes adrift, we find our way.
With every star, a story's cast,
In the galaxy's embrace, we're free at last.

Cosmic Cadence of Enchanted Light

In the realm where dreams reside,
Stars weave tales, as shadows bide.
Whispers dance on cosmic streams,
Illuminating all our dreams.

Nebulas swirl in colors bright,
Painting the canvas of the night.
Each sparkle sings a timeless song,
In this astral dance, we belong.

Wonders echo through the skies,
Where ancient magic never dies.
With every pulse, the universe sways,
Guiding us through the starry maze.

Crystals shimmer, shadows blend,
In this twilight, worlds transcend.
Bathed in hues of blue and gold,
The cosmic stories now unfold.

As we journey through this light,
Treading paths of pure delight.
Let every moment spark the night,
In the cadence of enchanted light.

Serenade of Twinkling Echoes

In the quiet space we find,
Twinkling whispers, sweetly kind.
Each echo wraps a tale of old,
A serenade of stories told.

Moonlight drapes the world in lace,
Drawing dreams to a gentle place.
Starlit notes float on the breeze,
Rustling through the ancient trees.

Harmony in the night sky,
Where constellations softly sigh.
Every shimmer sings of fate,
Inviting hearts to contemplate.

A lullaby from worlds afar,
Guides us like a shining star.
With melodies that twirl and twine,
In twinkling dance, our spirits shine.

Let the echoes fill the air,
In twilight's grace, without a care.
A serenade that lifts the soul,
Binding us to the universe whole.

Lost Melodies in Astral Waters

In the depths of cosmic seas,
Lost melodies float with ease.
Ripples shimmer, gently sway,
Guiding dreams that drift away.

Waves of harmony collide,
Secrets in the moon's soft tide.
Every note a distant sigh,
Whispers of the stars on high.

Echoes swimming, time unfolds,
In the stillness, tales are told.
The currents weave a tapestry,
Of forgotten songs, wild and free.

Floating gently in the night,
Searching for the lost delight.
In this realm of astral flow,
We'll uncover what we know.

With every stroke of starlit grace,
We shall find our rightful place.
In the waters deep and wide,
Lost melodies become our guide.

Ethereal Echoes of Tomorrow

In the dawn of what's to come,
Ethereal whispers, softly hum.
Veils of hope in shades of light,
Guide our hearts to take their flight.

Time unfolds its endless scroll,
As echoes shape the future's soul.
With every breath, we weave anew,
Dreams transform to vistas true.

Between the realms of What and Will,
A silent promise, waiting still.
In the dance of dawn and night,
Echoes of tomorrow ignite.

Colors blend in twilight's calm,
Stitching shadows, weaving balm.
Each note a seed of what may be,
In the fabric of destiny.

So let us sail on winds of change,
To lands where stars freely range.
In ethereal echoes, we find,
The tapestry of heart and mind.

Echoes of Prismatic Harmony

In realms where colors freely dance,
A spectrum sings, a dreamy trance.
Each note a whisper, soft and clear,
Embracing all who venture near.

The stars ignite in vibrant hues,
As melodies weave through twilight's blues.
With every breath the cosmos sighs,
Reflecting wonder in our eyes.

From crystal streams, the music flows,
A harmony only nature knows.
In echoes caught on silken air,
The heart finds peace, without a care.

In gardens bright, where shadows play,
The colors shift and gently sway.
Each petal hums, each leaf can sing,
In this, the joy the moments bring.

Where dreams and echoes intertwined,
In prismatic realms, I lost my mind.
For in the song of radiant light,
I found the magic of the night.

Whispers of Celestial Chords

Beneath the cloak of twinkling stars,
A cosmic tune ignites our scars.
Each strum, a tale of distant past,
In unity, the shadows cast.

With every chord, the universe bends,
As timeless tales and stardust blend.
A serenade to dreams unreal,
Awakening souls that dare to feel.

The moonlight weaves through midnight air,
Like gentle fingers, soft and rare.
With every note, the galaxies sigh,
Revealing secrets held on high.

In the silence, whispers rise,
Through ancient paths where wisdom lies.
Each echo calls from worlds unknown,
As harmony from dreams is grown.

In twilight's reach, the music plays,
A symphony of timeless days.
Where hearts entangle, spirits soar,
In celestial chords, forevermore.

Shards of a Luminous Melody

In prisms bright, where light is spun,
A melody, a race begun.
Each shard reflects a tale untold,
Of dreams and fears, of young and old.

With every note, a flicker glows,
Resonating where the magic flows.
In every fragment, beauty lies,
A brilliant dance beneath the skies.

The echoes form a tapestry,
Of swirling colors wild and free.
Each moment captured, crystal clear,
As memories linger ever near.

With harmonies that stretch and bend,
The universe, our wondrous friend.
It pulls us close, in tender grace,
As luminous shards we all embrace.

In radiant tones, our hearts align,
To feel the warmth of love divine.
For in the music, we are one,
A shining chorus 'neath the sun.

Glimmers in the Dusk

At dusk's embrace, when shadows blend,
A quiet calm begins to mend.
The world exudes a gentle light,
With whispers soft, the day takes flight.

From golden skies, the glimmers fall,
A tapestry to wrap us all.
Each shimmer echoes hopes untold,
A journey new, a hand to hold.

The twilight hums a sweet refrain,
Where dreams arise, and cares wane.
In every glow, a promise waits,
For new tomorrows, cherish fates.

As stars peek through the velvet night,
The glimmers twinkle, pure delight.
A hidden world, a secret keep,
Where souls can soar, where hearts can leap.

In dusk's embrace, we find our way,
With glimmers guiding through the gray.
For in the night, a truth we seek,
In fleeting moments, hearts will speak.

Unraveled Notes of a Celestial Song

In twilight's glow, a whisper weaves,
Notes dance lightly on the breeze,
Celestial dreams in silver threads,
Composing tales where silence treads.

Stars align in perfect rhyme,
Echoed secrets, lost in time,
A melody of night unfolds,
In moonlit skies, their grace beholds.

Within the heart, a chorus sings,
Of ancient hopes and longing things,
Each note a spark, each chord a flame,
In every heart, a whispered name.

The cosmos hums a lullaby,
As galaxies in silence lie,
Each twinkling star, a fleeting sound,
In harmony, their dreams are found.

So listen close, oh dreamer bright,
To songs that echo in the night,
For in this space, where shadows blend,
A symphony shall never end.

Whirlwinds of Shattered Sounds

In gusts of time, the echoes soar,
Whirlwinds call from yesteryore,
Fragments dance, both sharp and sweet,
In harmony, they twist and meet.

Through valleys deep, a storm unspools,
Scattering whispers, lost like jewels,
A clamor bold, yet soft with grace,
In every note, we find our place.

The curtains part, the shadows play,
In swirling hues of dusk and day,
A tempest's heart, a mournful song,
Where shattered dreams can still belong.

Each sorrow spins in perfect time,
With laughter steeped in dulcet chime,
The winds of change, they twist our fates,
Yet through it all, hope resonates.

So let the storms weave through the night,
For after darkness comes the light,
In whirlwinds bright, our souls will dance,
In shattered sounds, we find our chance.

Enchanted Waves of Distant Tone

On ocean's breath, a melody plays,
Enchanted waves in a dreamy haze,
A siren's call, both soft and deep,
In whispered lines, sweet secrets keep.

With every crest, a story flows,
Of distant lands where magic grows,
Each crashing wave a timeless tale,
In foamy swirls, our hearts set sail.

The sun dips low, the sky ignites,
With hues of violet, reds, and whites,
A tranquil hymn of twilight's bliss,
In salty air, we find our kiss.

As starlit paths unfurl above,
Each twinkling light, a sign of love,
We drift along, in dreams confined,
To distant tones that intertwine.

So close your eyes, let waves embrace,
In every echo, find your place,
For in the tide's soft, lulling tone,
Our souls are bound, we are not alone.

Soulful Strains from Cosmic Realms

From realms unknown, a voice can rise,
Soulful strains beneath the skies,
In cosmic echoes, truths align,
In stardust songs, our hopes entwine.

Through endless voids, the cadence flows,
Inviting all to lose their woes,
Each note a thread, each chord a guide,
In harmony's embrace, we bide.

The universe, with open arms,
Whispers softly, its ancient charms,
As galaxies twirl in rich designs,
The music of the heart defines.

So heed the call from far away,
Let rhythmic dreams and wishes sway,
Each soulful note a bridge of light,
In cosmic realms, we take our flight.

Awake the magic in your soul,
In melodies, find your whole,
For every strain leads to the dawn,
In timeless love, we shall move on.

Chasing Luminescent Shadows

In twilight's grasp, we chase the light,
Where wisps of dreams take daring flight.
Each flicker calls from realms unknown,
With echoes soft, our hearts have grown.

Amidst the trees, where whispers weave,
The shadows dance, we dare believe.
With every step, the night unfolds,
A tale of secrets yet untold.

The moonlight paints with silver threads,
Illuminating paths we tread.
With spark and flair, the starlit stream,
Guides us deeper into a dream.

Oh, chase the shadows, fleeting, bright,
In every corner, find the light.
For in the dark, a spark ignites,
And shadows twirl in endless nights.

So wander far, and do not fear,
For in the dark, the dawn is near.
With every glow, our spirits rise,
Chasing shadows 'neath painted skies.

The Melodies that Shatter

Upon the hill, the whispers cry,
A sound that weaves through silent sky.
Each note a thread, so frail, so vast,
Yet echoes linger from the past.

With breath withheld, we pause to hear,
The melodies that pull us near.
In every chord, a tale is spun,
Of battles lost and victories won.

Yet sometimes, in their fragile grace,
They fracture hearts and leave a trace.
The harmony that once was whole,
Now splinters deep within the soul.

So let the music fill the air,
With every rise, with every flare.
In shattering notes, we find our way,
Through broken dreams and bright array.

For from the shards, new songs will sing,
Transforming pain to vibrant spring.
Within the discord, strength will grow,
In melodies that ebb and flow.

Echoes in a Sunlit Abyss

Deep in the wood, where sunlight wanes,
Whispers linger, soft refrains.
In shadows deep, where secrets lie,
Echoes call, they never die.

The sun may rise, the dawn may glow,
But in the depths, the shadows flow.
Each echo sings of times gone by,
In vacuums vast, we learn to fly.

With shimmering grace, the light weaves through,
It dances bright, in colors true.
Yet darkness holds, an embrace so deep,
In the sunlit abyss, dreams sleep.

So listen close, for here resides,
The tales of ancient, watchful guides.
Each echo holds a story spun,
In realms where day and night are one.

And if you dare, beneath the gleam,
You'll find the heart of every dream.
For in the light, shadows persist,
In echoes sweet, the world exists.

Reflections of a Distant Melody

Upon the shore, waves softly sigh,
As distant songs drift through the sky.
Each note a promise, sweetly cast,
In gentle flows, our spirits blast.

With every swell and ebb of tide,
The melodies come from far and wide.
They whisper tales of lands unseen,
In harmony, we find our dream.

The stars above twinkle with grace,
As echoes dance in time and space.
Reflections shimmer on the sea,
A distant call, a memory.

So linger here, where waves embrace,
The music swirls in softest lace.
For in each note, a world awaits,
In distant lands and fated gates.

And when the dawn begins to break,
The melody will softly wake.
From distant shores, it calls our name,
In reflections clear, we find the same.

A Glance at the Infinite Harmony

In shadows deep where whispers roam,
A melody of stars finds home.
Each note a thread, a silken line,
Together weave, the grand design.

The night unfolds with shimmering grace,
As echoes dance in twilight's embrace.
Harmony hums through every heart,
Binding the worlds that drift apart.

With every breath, the cosmos sighs,
In sync beneath the endless skies.
A glimpse of truth in cosmic lore,
Revealing what we can't ignore.

The moonlight casts its gentle glow,
A whispered secret, soft and low.
Infinite whispers in the air,
Reminding us that we are rare.

So let us chase what's hard to find,
The symphony that moves the mind.
In unity, the stars align,
An orchestra of souls divine.

Constellations in Lyrical Silence

In silence deep, the stars awoke,
With tales entwined in starlit cloak.
Constellations weave their gentle plot,
In lyrical forms, a cosmic thought.

Each spark a wish, a dream set free,
Dancing softly for you and me.
In every twinkle lies a spark,
A secret shared in the night so dark.

The universe hums a tune so rare,
In rhythms woven through the air.
Through quiet moments, hearts will soar,
As dreams become what we explore.

Beneath the sky, we stand and gaze,
In wonderment, lost in a daze.
A lullaby from worlds afar,
Guiding us home, like a bright star.

Let the stillness wrap us tight,
In velvet shades of soft starlight.
Constellations pulse with stories told,
In the language of the bold.

Reflections of a Dreamt Symphony

In corridors where shadows play,
A symphony is born each day.
With chords that resonate through time,
In whispered tones, their voices climb.

Each note a glimpse of realms unknown,
Reflections of what we've outgrown.
In melody, we find our place,
A harmony that time can't erase.

The echoes linger, soft and light,
In memory's arms, they take flight.
A song that dances on the breeze,
Bringing comfort, urging ease.

Through every key, a tale unfolds,
Of whispered wishes, dreams retold.
Collectively, we breathe as one,
In the symphony of the sun.

Let the music guide our way,
In dreams where night dissolves to day.
With every heartbeat, we shall sing,
Reflections touched by everything.

Chasing the Luminous Pulse

In twilight's grasp, the world ignites,
A luminous dance through endless nights.
With every flicker that we chase,
The pulse of life brings forth its grace.

Stars pulse rhythmically on high,
Whispering secrets in the sky.
In fleeting moments, light takes form,
Guiding our hearts through the storm.

Across the heavens, dreams collide,
In shimmering paths, they gently glide.
Chasing echoes of what could be,
In the magic of eternity.

Let us run where shadows fade,
In the brilliance of the dreams we've made.
With every heartbeat, we ignite,
The luminous pulse of endless night.

So take my hand; together we'll fly,
Beyond the limits, toward the sky.
With every star, our spirits bloom,
Chasing light through the world's vast room.

Luminescent Puzzles of Sound

In twilight's hush, whispers start to rise,
Echoing tales from the starlit skies.
Notes dance like fireflies in the night,
Illuminating hearts with soft delight.

Invisible strings pull the world in tune,
While shadows waltz beneath the pale moon.
Every melody, a secret unfurled,
Binding us gently to a hidden world.

From whispers of breeze to thunder's roar,
The symphony swells, always wanting more.
Each sound a puzzle, crafted with care,
Unlocking mysteries hidden out there.

So, listen closely, let your spirit fly,
With every note, we'll learn how to sigh.
In the labyrinth where silence abounds,
We'll find our truth in these puzzles of sound.

And when the music fades, leaving its mark,
We'll cherish the echoes that dance in the dark.
For within this world where harmony plays,
Lives the magic of the brightest days.

Nostalgia of Distant Strains

A gentle breeze carries a song from afar,
Painting the skies with a silver star.
Each note a memory, soft as a sigh,
Whirling through hearts like whispers gone by.

In the hush of twilight, shadows are cast,
Echoes of laughter from a long-lost past.
Melodies murmur, weaving through time,
Bringing us back to the sweetest rhyme.

Waves of nostalgia crash on the shore,
As distant strains call us to explore.
Through the corridors of our restful dreams,
We dance with spirits, or so it seems.

Time may be fleeting, like leaves in the breeze,
Yet these haunting notes grant us sweet ease.
With each little flourish, we're carried away,
Into the embrace of a golden day.

The past is a treasure, a vibrant refrain,
Rooted in echoes that still entertain.
So hold on to rhythms that never shall fade,
For in distant strains, true love is laid.

The Rhapsody of Celestial Shards

Across the heavens, stars spark and gleam,
Composing a rhapsody, wild as a dream.
Celestial shards weave stories in light,
Guiding lost wanderers, igniting the night.

Each twinkle and shimmer, a note in the sky,
Telling of wonders that silently fly.
Gathering whispers from eons gone by,
Formatting symphonies heard in a sigh.

Galaxies turning, a dance in the void,
Songs of creation, both fragile and buoyed.
Infinity cradles the echoes of time,
Sculpting the cosmos in harmonious rhyme.

Listen intently to night's serenade,
For magic lies deep where dreams are made.
With every alignment of planets and stars,
We find our roots amidst the memoirs.

In the vast tapestry, we are but threads,
Driven by rhythms that spirit embeds.
So join in the chorus, let your heart flow,
In the rhapsody of celestial glow.

Melodies Woven in Starlight

Beneath the starlit cloak of night's embrace,
Melodies drift in a soft, tender grace.
Notes sprinkle down like drops of pure gold,
Telling of stories that are waiting to unfold.

In the tapestry spun with silvery thread,
Each chord plays softly, where thoughts dare to tread.
Dreams blend with whispers to craft the unseen,
Where hope takes its flight, forever serene.

Glowing like lanterns, the stars intertwine,
Creating a rhythm that's sacred, divine.
With every heartbeat, the cosmos aligns,
Embracing the echoes where magic entwines.

So let your soul soar on this gentle breeze,
As night's lullabies beg us to seize.
For in the stillness, together we find,
The melodies woven in starlight, unconfined.

Through whispers of time, we shall remain,
Guardians of dreams in a world untamed.
In starlit symphonies, we shall forever thrive,
For within these treasures, our hearts are alive.

Notes on a Woven Breeze

In whispers soft, the breezes play,
Carrying secrets of the day.
With every sigh, the leaves do dance,
As shadows twirl in nature's trance.

The sun dips low, a golden hue,
Casting dreams that feel so true.
A melody of chirps and hums,
Where time slows down, as twilight comes.

Each note a thread from hearts that yearn,
In quiet places, we discern.
With laughter woven through the air,
The world becomes a tapestry rare.

Oh, woven whispers, breeze of grace,
In every corner, find your place.
For in this dance of life's embrace,
We gather moments, swift and base.

Let not the night steal light away,
For magic softens shadows' sway.
Beneath the stars, the stories flow,
In woven breezes, love will grow.

Liquid Luminescence

In pools of light, reflections gleam,
As ripples dances in a dream.
The moonlight spills like silver wine,
Awakening secrets, softly divine.

Each droplet holds a universe,
A world within, diverse, diverse.
Where time stands still in liquid grace,
And echoes forge a sacred space.

With every wave that kisses shore,
A fleeting moment, evermore.
In luminous depths, our hopes ignite,
A beacon shining through the night.

The currents swirl with tales untold,
Of adventures bold, hearts uncontrolled.
In liquid luminescence bright,
We find our way through darkest night.

So let your spirit freely soar,
Embrace the magic at the core.
For in the flow of life's expanse,
We glide on waves, we dream, we dance.

Dissonance of the Heartfelt

In tangled chords, the heartbeats clash,
A symphony of love and ash.
Where pain and joy entwine and twine,
In shadows deep, the light will shine.

Each note a tear, each pause a sigh,
A fragile truth, a whispered cry.
With every clash, a path is forged,
In dissonance, our spirits surged.

Through heartbeats' drum, a tale unsung,
In rough-edged verses, we are strung.
With every note, we rise, we fall,
In messy bliss, we heed the call.

Though harmony may seem so far,
Within the discord lies our scar.
In every pang, a love so sweet,
A paradox beneath our feet.

So sing the songs of all we've missed,
Embrace the bitter with the blissed.
For in this dance of fractured art,
We find our strength, we mend the heart.

Serene Strains of Twilight

As daylight fades, serenity calls,
In gentle hues, the evening sprawls.
With purple skies and whispers low,
The world transforms, a tranquil show.

In twilight's arms, the shadows blend,
As day and night begin to mend.
A calm descends, soft as a sigh,
In moments captured, time drifts by.

The stars awaken, one by one,
While dreams take flight, our souls are spun.
With every twinkle, hope is born,
A quiet promise of the dawn.

In serene strains, the heartbeats hum,
A lullaby of what's to come.
The world finds rest, in peace resides,
In twilight's glow, true love abides.

So breathe the magic, hold it tight,
As day retreats, embrace the night.
For in this stillness, we take flight,
With whispers soft of love's delight.

Whispers of the Dazzling Echo

In twilight's glow, the whispers dance,
Secrets spoken, a fleeting chance.
With shadows weaving through the trees,
Wings of night sing soft decrees.

Moonbeams flicker, casting spells,
Magic stirs where silence dwells.
Echoes echo through the hues,
Lost in dreams like morning dew.

A distant laughter, faint and clear,
Calling soft, yet drawing near.
In every sigh, a story's thread,
Of wishes made, and dreams unsaid.

The stars respond, a twinkling tune,
Secrets kept beneath the moon.
Through the fabric of the night,
Magic flows, a soft delight.

Together in this sparkly realm,
Where every whisper finds its helm.
A dazzling echo, bathed in light,
Guiding souls through endless flight.

Shimmering Notes in Twilight

In twilight's arms, the world sighs sweet,
Each note a dream, a heartbeat's beat.
Silver strings of fate entwine,
Melodies of dusk divine.

Beneath the boughs where shadows creep,
Whispers weave, the secrets keep.
Stars emerge, like notes on high,
A symphony for every eye.

Harmony sways in the velvet air,
A dance of light beyond compare.
Every shimmer a tale retold,
Of brave hearts, and spirits bold.

Music ripples through the glen,
A fleeting magic, time and again.
Eclipsed in wonder, dreams take flight,
In shimmering notes of the twilight.

As darkness drapes in tender folds,
The night reveals what light enfolds.
In every shimmer, a spark ignites,
A timeless waltz beneath the lights.

A Cadence of Broken Dreams

In the echoes of the lingering past,
Dreams like paper, fragile, fast.
Whispers tattooed on weary night,
A cadence born of lost delight.

Fragments glisten, scattered wide,
Hopes and wishes, bated tide.
Time weaves tales, both fierce and meek,
Searching voices yearn to speak.

In the shadows where shadows blend,
Yearning hearts mend what they send.
Through the cracks, the daylight streams,
A symphony of broken dreams.

For every silence, a voice will rise,
Unfolding truths in disguise.
Threads of light stitch every seam,
In this cadence of broken dreams.

A rhythm echoes, bittersweet,
Walking paths where shadows meet.
In every heartbeat, a wish anew,
A cadence calling to me and you.

Harmony amidst the Glare

In the clamor of the bustling day,
Harmony hides, tucked away.
In the glare of ambition's fight,
A gentle tune glimmers bright.

Amidst the rush, where few may pause,
Notes of peace stir without cause.
A symphony ringing, pure and clear,
Inviting souls to draw near.

With every flicker, chaos bends,
Calmness lingers, as twilight descends.
In hidden corners, melodies soar,
An echo of life, forevermore.

Whispers weave through the busy throng,
A silent hymn, both soft and strong.
When the world turns harsh and bare,
Find your harmony amidst the glare.

Listen close, the notes will rise,
Painting wonders across the skies.
In every heartbeat, find the flare,
For harmony waits in the glare.

Chords of Dappled Light

In a glen where shadows play,
Sunbeams dance, then stray,
Whispers in the leaves' embrace,
A melody of nature's grace.

Birds sing softly up above,
Caught in pools of light and love,
Every note a gentle sigh,
As time unraveled, drifting by.

Mossy stones beneath our feet,
Fragmented tunes, bittersweet,
Glow like stars in daylight's hue,
A symphony born anew.

The brook hums a secret song,
Rushing past, it flows along,
Reflecting dreams in every stream,
A vision wrapped in golden gleam.

Twilight brings a softer air,
With twilight songs beyond compare,
In shadows deep, where we belong,
We find our place, and sing along.

Eclipsed in Sound and Fury

Amidst the storm, the tempest roars,
The world shakes, as thunder soars,
In chaos found, a fierce delight,
A dance of shadows in the night.

Winds howl fierce, like spirits freed,
Rage and calm, a tangled creed,
In echoes deep, a wild lament,
Each heartbeat felt, each breath spent.

Lightning cuts the sky in two,
A fleeting flash, a moment true,
Between the bursts, time stands still,
Fury tempered by iron will.

The rain drums hard, a fevered sound,
A symphony that knows no bound,
Beneath the veil of stormy night,
We find our strength, we find our light.

Through sound and fury, we ascend,
The chaos bends but will not end,
In every cry, hope we trace,
A glimmer bright in dark's embrace.

Luminous Inspirations from the Past

In dusty tomes, the wisdom sleeps,
Echoes of voices that time keeps,
Pages flutter, stories told,
Whispers of dreams in the gold.

Once bright eyes danced with fire,
Fingers traced each great desire,
Unraveling tales of loves once lost,
The price of dreams, the human cost.

With every word, a heart revealed,
Secrets of time slowly unsealed,
In shadows cast by moon's soft light,
We seek the truth that knows no night.

The past weaves threads through every line,
Binding moments with love divine,
Inspired souls haunt every page,
Filling life with spirit, sage.

So let the stories guide our way,
In luminous night, in break of day,
For every spark from those before,
Creates new light forevermore.

Echoing Spheres of Tranquility

In the garden where silence sings,
Harmony in gentle wings,
Petals rest on emerald blades,
Each breath a peace that never fades.

Beneath the boughs, the stillness grows,
In whispered tales, the quiet flows,
Time drips slow, like morning dew,
A lullaby, both old and new.

Clouds drift soft along the sky,
Each one a secret passing by,
With every breeze, tranquility,
Unraveled threads of memory.

Fragrant blooms in colors rare,
Invite our hearts to linger there,
In petals' fold, the world stands still,
A tranquil heart, a tranquil will.

Through echoes sweet, our spirits soar,
In spheres of calm, forevermore,
For in this space, we come to see,
The vastness of our harmony.

A Serenade in Shattered Glass

In twilight's grip, the whispers sigh,
Fragments of dreams in the night sky.
A melody lost in crystal shards,
Casting shadows, playing guards.

Each note a shard, each beat a tear,
Echoing tales of love and fear.
Windows broken, yet hearts remain,
Yearning still in the softest rain.

Beneath the moon, reflections gleam,
A serenade born from a broken dream.
The echoes dance, the stories weave,
In every shard, a world to believe.

Through the silence, the soft winds play,
Carving pathways where dreams may stray.
With each glance, lost pieces sing,
A song of hope the night will bring.

So gather the shards, let spirits fly,
In shattered glass, we learn to try.
For in each crack, a story's told,
A serenade of hearts, brave and bold.

The Echo of Starlight's Kiss

Under the cloak of night's embrace,
Whispers of starlight softly trace.
A kiss so gentle, a spark divine,
In the folds of silence, shadows entwine.

Each twinkle tells of distant dreams,
A symphony crafted in silvery beams.
Where wishes wander, lost in time,
A rhythm pulsing in celestial rhyme.

In cosmic halls, the echoes play,
Guiding lost souls who drift away.
Through velvet skies, the stories gleam,
A tapestry woven of midnight dreams.

Listen closely, hear the call,
In the quiet brilliance, we find it all.
A starlit dance beneath our feet,
The echo of kisses, bittersweet.

So hold your breath, let wonder stay,
In the hush of night, come what may.
For starlight whispers to those who dare,
An echo of love in the cool night air.

Sparks in the Silence

In the depths of night, where shadows loom,
Sparks arise from the stillness' gloom.
A flicker bright, a moment caught,
In silence, a world of wonders sought.

Amidst the quiet, hearts entwine,
In the space between, a spark divine.
Words unspoken, yet deeply felt,
In every breath, a magic dwelt.

Glimmers dance in the dusky air,
Whispers of secrets, moments rare.
Through the dark, the flashes fly,
Igniting stories, time slips by.

So tread lightly on this sacred ground,
Where sparks of joy can still be found.
For in the silence, worlds collide,
A tapestry woven with love as guide.

Let heartbeats pulse like fires aglow,
In the quiet places, let feelings flow.
For in the stillness, life ignites,
Sparks in the silence, magical nights.

Dreamscapes of Harmonious Echoes

In dreamscapes vast, where echoes roam,
Harmonies rise, creating a home.
A canvas painted with twilight's grace,
Where every heartbeat finds its place.

Through vibrant hues, the visions glow,
In the labyrinth of thoughts, we flow.
A serenade sung by the stars above,
In every note, a whisper of love.

Breathe in the essence of sacred night,
With every flicker, hearts take flight.
Through shadowed paths, let kindness lead,
In dreamscapes woven, a heart's true seed.

So journey boldly through realms unknown,
In the tapestry where dreams are sown.
With echoes guiding, let spirits soar,
In harmonious symphonies, forevermore.

For in this realm of endless delight,
We find the spark to light the night.
With dreamscapes calling, we rise and blend,
In echoes of magic, there's no end.

The Interlude of Glimmering Hues

In twilight's grasp, the colors blend,
A canvas vast, where dreams ascend.
Each hue a tale, each shade a sigh,
Beneath the stars that softly lie.

Whispers travel on the breeze,
Through leaves that shimmer, dance with ease.
The world a palette, bright and wide,
Where secrets of the heart reside.

Sunset's glow, a fleeting kiss,
In moments like these, we find our bliss.
Compassion blooms in golden light,
As shadows fade with the coming night.

In glimmers soft, our hopes ignite,
A tapestry of day and night.
Each flicker holds the promise near,
A symphony for all to hear.

So linger here, in shades that play,
As daylight slowly slips away.
For in this interlude so dear,
Our souls connect, our path is clear.

Mosaics of Shimmering Resonance

The world unfolds in mosaic dreams,
Curated whispers, soft moonbeams.
A patchwork life of joy and woe,
In each small fragment, stories grow.

Glimmers of laughter, tears that shine,
Interwoven fates, yours and mine.
Each piece a moment, every breath,
In vibrant echoes that defy death.

Cobblestones beneath our feet,
Resonate with tales discreet.
In silent spaces, bonds we weave,
As night embraces, hearts believe.

Colors merge, a dance of sound,
In every corner, magic found.
From laughter's sparkle to sorrow's sigh,
These shimmering threads will never die.

So gather close, and hear the call,
In this mosaic, we rise or fall.
Each heartbeat shared, a melody,
In shimmering resonance, we're free.

Unbroken Dreams

Upon the hill where shadows play,
Unbroken dreams find light of day.
A tender hope ignites the sky,
As starlit wishes dare to fly.

Each thought a spark, a flame within,
That battles doubt, that fights to win.
With every heartbeat, every sigh,
They whisper softly, 'You can try.'

In valleys low, where fears may dwell,
These dreams will rise, they'll weave a spell.
A tapestry of light and shade,
In every heart, their magic laid.

Through darkest nights, they gently guide,
Reminding us of what's inside.
For in the depths of silent screams,
There lies the pulse of unbroken dreams.

So chase the light, let shadows fade,
Embrace the journey that we've made.
For dreams, though tested, find their way,
To blossom bright, come what may.

Echoed Songs

A melody of whispered notes,
In twilight's glow, the sweet sound floats.
Out in the woods, they call our name,
Echoed songs, a haunting flame.

Underneath the silver skies,
Where every sound, a treasure lies.
The rustling leaves, the bubbling stream,
All harmonize in nature's dream.

Each bird's sweet chant, a memory,
Bringing forth the heart's decree.
In every breath, in every tune,
Life's vibrant pulse beneath the moon.

As shadows dance, the echoes swell,
In every heart, their stories tell.
A concert shared, our spirits strong,
A universe within this song.

So close your eyes, and let it flow,
These echoed songs will help us grow.
For in each note, we find our place,
In harmony, through time and space.

Synthesis of Crystalline Whispers

In secret rooms where silence glows,
Crystalline whispers softly rose.
A synthesis of all we crave,
From hidden depths, our minds we save.

Through fragile shards of shattered dreams,
We gather light in flowing streams.
Each whisper holds a truth so rare,
A magic spun from hope and care.

Like diamonds birthed from darkened night,
Their beauty glistens, pure and bright.
In every voice, a spark ignites,
Connecting hearts through endless nights.

In echoes soft, our stories blend,
A tapestry that will not end.
Through shifting shades, in every space,
Crystalline whispers find their place.

So listen close, and let them guide,
These gentle tones will never hide.
For in their song, we come alive,
In synthesis, we shall survive.

Fleeting Chords of Light

In twilight's embrace, shadows play,
A whisper of dusk ends the day.
Stars flicker softly, a fleeting spark,
Guiding lost souls through the dark.

Echoes of laughter swirl in the air,
Secrets of night brushed with care.
Light dances lightly on whispering streams,
Chasing the remnants of timeless dreams.

Each glimmer a story, each shimmer a song,
A tapestry woven, where spirits belong.
Through flickering shadows, the heart may soar,
Finding the magic that's hidden in lore.

With every pulse, the silence breaks,
As shimmering light, the darkness shakes.
In the hush of the moment, we linger near,
Chords of the cosmos strum sweet and clear.

Let us embrace these fleeting cues,
In cosmic concerts, we find the muse.
For in every heartbeat, every bright glow,
Lie fleeting chords of light, we must follow.

Glimmers from the Silent Orchestra

In the quiet of dawn, the world takes a breath,
An orchestra stirs, free from death.
Strings woven softly, a gentle refrain,
Melodies carried on whispers of rain.

Each drop a note in the grand symphony,
Harmony floats through the realms of the free.
Glimmers arise from shadows cast wide,
Echoing dreams where the heart cannot hide.

The wind carries tunes from the heavens above,
Brushed with the essence of tumultuous love.
With every heartbeat, the silence reveals,
A symphony woven with unspoken feels.

Softly they shimmer, like stars in the night,
A canvas of sound, sapphire and white.
Through alleys of sound, they twirl and they sway,
Glimmers from silence, they guide the way.

So hush now, listen, for music is near,
In glimmers of twilight, its message is clear.
The silent orchestra calls us to play,
In notes that will linger, then gently drift away.

Celestial Whirlwinds of Sound

In the vastness of skies, where stardust whirls,
Celestial winds weave through cosmic pearls.
A trumpet sounds forth, in spirals it sings,
Bringing to life all the dreams of kings.

Each roar of the nebula, vibrant and bold,
Is a tale of the cosmos eternally told.
Whirlwinds of sound crash like waves on the shore,
Painting the silence with music galore.

Amidst the expanse, where no boundaries bind,
Notes from the heavens drift through the mind.
In dances of beauty, the universe twirls,
Whispers of wonder in starlit swirls.

Listen intently, let your spirit fly,
With celestial music, embrace the sky.
By harmonies grand and cadences bright,
The universe beckons in shimmering light.

With each cosmic gust, let your heart be found,
In celestial whirlwinds of ancient sound.
For here in the music, we're never alone,
In the vastness of space, we all are home.

Dances of Mist and Sparkle

In the morning's blush, the fog gently sways,
Dancing like sprites in a shimmering maze.
Mist twirls around in a delicate trance,
Inviting the light for a wondrous dance.

Each droplet of dew, a crystalline cheer,
Catching the sunlight that wanders near.
Colors explode in this ethereal ballet,
As magic unfolds at the break of day.

Whispers of stories hidden in grey,
Dances of dreams that softly sway.
With every step on this enchanted stage,
Life weaves its tale, turning each page.

Through veils of enchantment, our spirits entwine,
In dances of mist, where moments align.
With sparkles a-glow, like stars in our eyes,
We revel in magic beneath boundless skies.

So join in the dance, let your heart take flight,
In the whispers of mist, find solace and light.
For every soft sparkle and twirl's sweet embrace,
Teaches us beauty in this sacred space.

Resonance of Forgotten Notes

In whispers lost, the echoes dwell,
A symphony of dreams to tell.
Each note a tale of yesteryear,
In twilight's hush, we pause and hear.

The moonlight dances on the strings,
Reviving hope that silence brings.
With every chord, the shadows play,
A melody that fades away.

Forgotten songs in twilight's grasp,
We chase the echoes, yearn to clasp.
Yet time erases, one by one,
The notes of laughter, joy, and fun.

In silence deep, a memory stirs,
The heartache sings, though never blurs.
Like stars that fade beyond the night,
Their resonance is pure delight.

And in that space where dreams reside,
Those whispered notes no longer hide.
They rise again, through tears and fears,
A harmony throughout the years.

Tapestry of Shattered Light

Woven threads in midnight's loom,
Colors lost, now weave in bloom.
A tapestry of glint and glow,
Where secrets hide and shadows flow.

Fragments scatter, a fleeting spark,
In every corner, whispers hark.
Shattered lanterns, glow like stars,
Illuminate our hidden scars.

Crimson threads entwined with gold,
Stories of the brave and bold.
Each stitch a promise, each tear a sigh,
A map of journeys that never die.

Through shattered light, we see the whole,
Every fragment feeds the soul.
The beauty lies in what we find,
In tangled dreams of heart and mind.

So let the fibers intertwine,
Create a world that feels divine.
In this mosaic, forged from strife,
We find the magic, we find our life.

Dappled Frequencies at Dawn

As morning breaks through whispered haze,
Light unfolds its golden rays.
In dappled hues, the world awakes,
Each moment sweet, the heart it takes.

The breeze carries a gentle song,
A melody where we belong.
The frequencies of daybreak chime,
In sync, we dance through sands of time.

Birds take flight in honeyed skies,
Their joyous calls a soft reprise.
The earth exhales, a breath renewed,
In nature's grace, we find our muse.

Through shadows cast by waking trees,
Each leaf in turn begins to tease.
The dappled light, so full of grace,
Reflects the hope in every face.

Awake, arise and greet the morn,
In every breath, a dream reborn.
Let frequencies in harmony play,
And guide us through this brand new day.

Sonnet of the Shimmering Veil

A veil of dreams, so soft and light,
It sways between the day and night.
In silver threads, the wishes twine,
Reflecting hope, both yours and mine.

With every shimmer, stories glide,
Across the realms where spirits bide.
In whispered secrets softly spun,
A tapestry of two as one.

The veil reveals a world untold,
Where mysteries of the heart unfold.
In shades of twilight, grace prevails,
Through windswept paths, the heart embales.

So let us dance where dreams collide,
In shimmering light, our souls confide.
With each heartbeat, we shall unveil,
The magic found in love's soft trail.

Embrace the light that guides our way,
Through every shadow, night or day.
A sonnet penned in starlit grace,
In every pause, our hearts will trace.

Sharded Harmonies of Ancient Wisdom

In twilight whispers, secrets unfold,
Each shard of wisdom, stories retold.
Echoes of ancients in twilight's embrace,
Guiding the seekers to find their own place.

Stars glimmer softly, a celestial map,
Drawing the curious, luring the hap.
With every heartbeat, a lesson to glean,
In the sharded harmonies, truths can be seen.

A tapestry woven of night and of light,
Holding together both shadow and bright.
In troubled waters, stillness reveals,
The strength of the spirit, the power it yields.

Threads of connection, across time they bind,
Uniting the hearts and the ever-curious mind.
In every question, the answers reside,
As ancient wisdom becomes our guide.

So seek the fragments with open intent,
In the heart of the echoes, be ever content.
For sharded harmonies call out to thee,
A symphony woven, forever to be.

Celestial Play in Shimmering Nights

Under the veil of soft diamond skies,
The cosmos dances, bright laughter flies.
Moonlight beckons in silken hues,
As dreams take flight on the evening muse.

Stars play together in a rhythmic sway,
Whispering wishes, guiding the way.
Galaxies twirl in an endless embrace,
With every heartbeat, they quicken the pace.

Creation's canvas, painted in spark,
Illuminating journeys that venture in dark.
The universe sighs, a soft lullaby,
In celestial play, where nightbirds fly.

Time is but sand in the hourglass spun,
Moments like fireflies—each a small sun.
With every flicker, a promise is made,
In shimmering nights, where dreams are laid.

So dance with the stars, let your spirit soar,
In the play of the heavens, forever explore.
For the night is a treasure, rich and bright,
In the celestial realms of shimmering light.

Songs woven through the Veil

Beneath the surface, a river does flow,
With songs of the shadows, hidden and low.
Threads of the past in the present entwined,
A tapestry woven for hearts to find.

The veil between worlds is thin as a sigh,
Where echoes linger and spirits reply.
Every note carries the weight of the years,
A symphony crafted from laughter and tears.

In moments of silence, the music breaks free,
A chorus of voices, haunting with glee.
The stories of ages illuminate night,
As songs through the veil dance in pure light.

With every refrain, a spark of old flame,
Invoking the whispers, invoking their name.
Woven together, the threads softly gleam,
In songs through the veil, where all souls dream.

So listen, dear traveler, to what you can hear,
In the hush of the night, let your heart steer.
For songs woven through the veil will inspire,
With love and with magic, igniting the fire.

Celestial Notes adrift in Time

Floating on echoes, the stars softly sing,
Melodies woven from the light they bring.
In the stillness of night, they drift and they glide,
Celestial notes on an endless tide.

Time bends and sways like a gentle breeze,
Each moment a note in the cosmic keys.
Harmonies linger, in shadows they play,
Cradled by silence in an endless ballet.

Dreams ride the currents of moons and suns,
Chasing the whispers, where magic runs.
Every heartbeat draws us closer to find,
The celestial notes drifting through time.

In this quiet space, the universe swirls,
In numbers and rhythms, bright wonders unfurl.
The dance of the cosmos, forever sublime,
With celestial notes adrift in time.

So let your soul soar in the dark of the night,
Embrace the unknown, follow your light.
For in the great expanse where horizons meet,
Celestial notes echo, bringing joy sweet.

Kaleidoscope of Distant Harmonies

In twilight's gentle, whispering hue,
Colors blend, a magical view.
Soft echoes of laughter fill the air,
As dreams dance lightly, free from care.

Glimmers of starlight trace the night,
Their secrets woven, pure delight.
A symphony calls from afar,
Guiding lost souls like a bright star.

Each note twirls in the zephyr's embrace,
Unfolding stories with delicate grace.
Together they weave, diverge, then unite,
In eternal harmony, boundless and bright.

Through shadows and light, the heart shall play,
A kaleidoscope of night and day.
With every heartbeat, a melody flows,
In the garden where imagination grows.

So let us wander where magic sings,
In the embrace of all wondrous things.
For in the distance, a harmony's tune,
Awaits beneath the warm silver moon.

With colors that shift, in dreams we shall fly,
Embracing the world with a hopeful sigh.
In the kaleidoscope of our shared refrain,
Together we'll dance through joy and through pain.

The Silent Crescendo

In the quiet, a whisper unfolds,
Stories untold in shadows so bold.
Like fragile glass caught in the light,
Echoes of moments take flight.

The heart beats softly, a muted drum,
A melody stirs, yet feels so numb.
Waves of longing crash on the shore,
As silence beckons for something more.

Every breath carries a weight of dreams,
Woven together in fine silver seams.
While time slips gently, like sand through hands,
A symphony grows in faraway lands.

The air thickens with notes left unsaid,
In the space between hearts, a thread.
We lean into silence, drawing near,
The crescendo builds, yet no one can hear.

So hush now, and listen to the night,
For in the stillness, we find our light.
In the silent crescendo, our spirits soar,
Binding us tightly forevermore.

As the stars bear witness, our souls align,
In whispers of hope, our hearts entwine.
In the quiet embrace, let our passion grow,
For in this silence, true stories will flow.

Rhapsody of the Unseen

In twilight's cloak, the magic begins,
Soft rustles and murmurs, as day thins.
The unseen realm dances close by,
Wrapped in the shroud of a dusky sky.

With every flicker, the whispers ignite,
A rhapsody echoes, both wild and bright.
Like tendrils of smoke in the midnight air,
Unfolding secrets, unraveling care.

The unseen thread binds the hearts of the lost,
Weaving through shadows, no matter the cost.
A tapestry rich, with laughter and fears,
In the fabric of dreams, embroidered with tears.

So dance in the dark where the wild spirits roam,
In the rhapsody's heartbeat, we'll find our home.
With every shared glance, the night's song shines,
Uniting our souls in invisible lines.

Through the veil of the night, we glide like a breeze,
Swaying together, lost in sweet ease.
For the unseen is where the truest love dwells,
In a rhapsody wrapped in soft, whispered spells.

So close your eyes to all that is shown,
And listen to the magic, the seeds we have sown.
In the heart of the unseen, we know we'll be free,
For the rhapsody lives in you and in me.

Illumination in Broken Measures

In fragments of light, a dance takes flight,
Moments of clarity pierce the night.
Through shattered mirrors, visions collide,
Finding the truth we try to hide.

Each fractured step, a story unfolds,
In the silence, the heart boldly scolds.
The beauty in chaos begins to gleam,
Revealing the essence of every dream.

Let shadows embrace what always has been,
In the cracks of the world, love slips in.
With colors that flicker in soft, gentle hues,
Illumination painted by somber muse.

In broken measures, the song finds its way,
Dancing through doubts, in sweet disarray.
For in every stumble, there lies a chance,
To rise from the ashes and bravely dance.

So gather the pieces, let light pierce through,
In every misstep lies something new.
With hearts wide open, we learn to embrace,
Illumination found in our human grace.

Through all that is broken, we'll craft a refrain,
Filling the silence, extinguishing pain.
In the beauty of flaws, our stories combine,
Illumination discovered, perfectly divine.

The Breath of the Universe

In the hush of night, stars intertwine,
Whispers of ages in cosmic design.
Galaxies dance in a vibrant whirl,
Wonders unfurl in a timeless swirl.

Each twinkling light a story untold,
Of dreams and secrets in shadows of gold.
Echoes of stardust in silence draw near,
Embrace of the cosmos, eternal and clear.

In the vast expanse, emotions align,
Bound by the threads of space and divine.
Through nebulae spun from celestial threads,
The breath of the universe quietly spreads.

Where myths and reality intertwine,
Infinite journeys through realms we define.
In the cradle of time, we find our way,
Guided by starlight, come night or day.

As whispers of twilight embrace the dawn,
Hope lingers on, though the night is long.
For in the vast calm, we all can ignite,
The breath of the universe, pure and bright.

Melodies in the Mist

In the valley where shadows play,
Melodies in mist drift away.
Soft as a sigh, sweet as a dream,
Nature's own song, a soft-spoken theme.

Hidden hints in the morning dew,
Chords of the earth, so fresh and new.
A rustle of leaves, a gentle breeze,
Whispers of secrets among the trees.

Each note suspended in time's gentle grace,
Echoing softly in a tranquil space.
Harmony woven through twilight's thread,
In every heartbeat, where stories are spread.

Through valleys and hills, the music flows,
A tapestry rich where the wild wind blows.
In the embrace of fog, dreams start to rise,
Melodies hidden beneath muted skies.

Let your spirit dance with the dusk's gentle glow,
In the symphony vast where the soft shadows flow.
Embrace the enchantment that nature imparts,
For in the mist's lullaby, we find our hearts.

Paths of Enchanted Sounds

Beneath the twilight, whispers arise,
Paths of enchanted sounds, hidden ties.
Footsteps echo on cobblestone streets,
Where magic and melody softly meet.

In forests alive with twilight's hum,
A chorus of owls, a night-time drum.
Crickets compose under starlit skies,
Each note a treasure, where wonder lies.

Through shimmering trails, we wander and weave,
Searching for echoes that fate may conceive.
The wind carries tales of lost delight,
In paths of the night, where dreams take flight.

Every rustle and whisper invites us near,
To dance through the shadows, to conquer our fear.
In every heartbeat, the world sings along,
A tapestry woven from stories and song.

As shadows lengthen and daylight fades,
In enchanted paths, where the spirit wades,
Let the music guide you through realms so wide,
For the heart knows the way, if you let it decide.

Glinting Echoes of Eternity

In the quiet of dusk, memories gleam,
Glinting echoes of eternity dream.
Time intertwines like a river's flow,
Whispers of ages in moonlight's glow.

Where moments are captured, still and bright,
Fragments of laughter in soft, gentle light.
The memory's touch, like a silken thread,
Weaves tales of the future and paths that we've tread.

In starlit embrace, where time stands still,
Each heartbeat echoing with fervor and will.
The past winks slyly from shadows of night,
In glinting echoes, we reach for the light.

Through the corridors of history's breath,
Life dances boldly with love and with death.
In the tapestry woven with threads so fine,
Each glimmer a promise, each shimmer divine.

So gather the whispers, let them unfold,
Embrace the echoes, both tender and bold.
For in every glint lies a story in wait,
Echoes of eternity shaping our fate.

Refractions of Requiem

In shadows deep, the whispers wane,
A ghostly echo, a fading strain.
With whispered dreams that softly part,
The memory clings to the aching heart.

Each note, a tear in twilight's song,
In hollow halls where lost souls long.
Reflections dance on the edge of light,
An elegy etched in the coming night.

Rays of sorrow, like fractured glass,
Scatter the echoes as moments pass.
A requiem sung for the fallen years,
In every silence, a stream of tears.

Within the mist, forgotten time,
Threads of fate in a woven rhyme.
We seek the dawn, yet dusk prevails,
In a world that mourns, as stillness veils.

Let us hold close what once was bright,
In the splintered shards of fading light.
We craft a song from aches that bore,
In refractions lost, we seek for more.

Resonance of Forgotten Chimes

Beneath the bells of yesteryear,
Whispers linger, soft yet clear.
Time, a tapestry, woven tight,
Hums the stories of day and night.

Chimes that echo through shadowed streets,
Call back the faces of past heartbeats.
In the quiet dusk, they softly play,
In melodies lost, they seem to sway.

Each tone a secret, deep and wise,
Reflecting dreams in starlit skies.
Resonance woven in ancient glade,
Where memories dance, and shadows fade.

Let us listen to the songs of branches,
In rustling leaves, fate's tender chances.
In forgotten sounds that entwine the air,
Find the warmth of love lingering there.

For in each chime, a tale derides,
Lost in the echoes where hope abides.
A harmony resonates through the night,
In whispers soft, and the fading light.

Ethereal Symphony of Wandering Hearts

In the stillness, lost souls awake,
With every heartbeat, a path they take.
An ethereal tune that calls them near,
As stardust weaves through the tapestries sheer.

Wandering hearts in the moon's embrace,
Seek the glow of a forgotten place.
In harmony's breath, they drift like dreams,
Through the shadows of whispered themes.

The symphony flows with the river's might,
In currents of memory, they take flight.
Each note, a brushstroke of dusk and dawn,
In vivid colors, their spirits drawn.

Connected softly like stars' gentle blaze,
In the universe's timeless gaze.
They dance on the wind in spirals bright,
An endless song in the velvet night.

For every heart has a symphony's call,
A melody shared when the night does fall.
Let the wandering embrace the unknown,
In the ethereal tunes, they are never alone.

Crescendo in a Splintered World

In fractured echoes the silence slips,
A crescendo building in whispered tips.
Amidst the chaos, hope still dares,
As hearts unite in the weighty airs.

Shattered dreams, like glass, reflect,
Fleeting moments, to love connect.
Amidst the clash, a rhythm found,
In tangled chords, we are spellbound.

From the ruins rise the voices strong,
In unison, we find our song.
Notes that soar and gently wane,
In every struggle, there beats a flame.

A splintered world yet gleams with grace,
As we gather pieces, our rightful place.
With every heartbeat, the dream ascends,
In the crescendo, love never ends.

So let the music pulse anew,
In a tapestry woven with every hue.
In this harmony, we stand entwined,
In a world reborn, our hearts aligned.

www.ingramcontent.com/pod-product-compliance
Ingram Content Group UK Ltd.
Pitfield, Milton Keynes, MK11 3LW, UK
UKHW022037040225
4445UKWH00034B/381